Leadership
WISDOM

A Guide to Producing Extraordinary Results

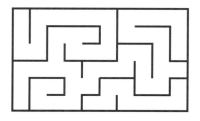

Larry L. Liberty, Ph.D.

Dedication

For over forty years of my life my mother, Athyl Crowder Liberty, has been an inspiration and encouragement to me. Through good and bad times she has steadfastly shown her love, patience, and caring. She is one of those rare people who attracts everyone, is generous to a fault, and is unstoppable in the face of difficulties. This book is dedicated to her and all the extraordinary forms of wisdom which she has shown and modeled for me through these many years.

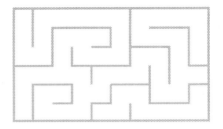

TABLE OF CONTENTS

Leadership WISDOM

Executives, managers, and supervisors are under attack. From every corner and direction they are assaulted by new and growing demands. They work in both the private and the public sector. They are men and women who have good intentions and insufficient resources. Their commitment is constantly challenged — their authority is in steady remission. A typical day will include some, if not all, of these mandates:

- ▶ Decrease the size of staff without decreasing the results that are needed
- ▶ Reduce the amount of time needed to deliver a product or service
- ▶ Deal with increasingly complex personnel issues
- ▶ Resolve issues of race, diversity and preference
- ▶ Re-engineer or redesign work processes
- ▶ Increase customer satisfaction
- ▶ Increase employee satisfaction
- ▶ Increase profit and productivity
- ▶ Decrease the cost of doing business
- ▶ Ensure the growth and development of staff
- ▶ Grow and develop yourself
- ▶ Stay sane
- ▶ Try to survive until the next buy-out or retirement

Perhaps this is a travesty or perhaps it is just part of the inevitable cycle of life that is part of business and the world. In either case, we call upon these courageous women and men who are supervisors, managers, and executives. We summon them to produce extraordinary results in the midst of it all. We invite them to bring about miracles as if they were trained in magic. And, for the most part, they succeed in some fashion or other.

But there are a few who excel in the midst of this chaos. There are a few who somehow use these circumstances and conditions to find something extraordinary within themselves. These people not only produce extraordinary results but do it without damaging themselves or their fellow employees. In fact their staffs often prosper and grow in the middle of all the confusion and disorder.

And what quality is present amongst these few exceptional people? What comes into play that allows the unusual and unpredictable to happen when most can barely survive? It is something that is difficult to teach and impossible to force — WISDOM.

What a strange word to apply to managing and to the world of business. But clearly it is appropriate, for we have all met someone who has this uncanny ability to pierce through the fog of difficulties and complexities, and get to the heart of what is wanted and needed.

We have been surprised at how some people are unflappable while we are frenzied and insane due to the same set of events. We have wondered at how we are suddenly confused while another is incredibly clearheaded at the same moment. This is wisdom in action.

Webster's Dictionary defines "wisdom" as:

"the quality . . . and faculty of making the best use of knowledge, experience, understanding; having the power to discern and judge correctly; . . . able to discriminate between what is true and what is false, proper and improper . . ."

Image how having these qualities separates one from the rest of the people who are simply trying to get by or to **survive**. Wisdom is this remarkable quality of being able to get access to information and data, and to make decisions from what is true rather than what is just perceived or apparent.

And so, in our daily work conditions, our supervisors, managers, and executives are asked to bring this Wisdom into play. And we ask them to do so without knowing what we're really asking. And we ask them to do so without a clue as to how to develop it, expand it, or even uncover it. These people are, for the most part, on their own.

Well, this book is going to help. People who have this quality of being wise, perceptive, insightful, discerning and judicious have, unconsciously for the most part, a model that gives them access to this wisdom. My team has watched, studied, and observed some of the most successful supervisors, managers, and executives from businesses and corporations, and has distilled this process into a model. This model is designed to allow you, the reader, to begin to develop the patterns and tendencies needed to access your own wisdom.

Clearly, wisdom is an internal process. For the most part wisdom, as such, takes years to develop. But the process that gives rise to wisdom is available to you — here and now. I hope that this book contributes to your growth and development, deepens your wisdom, and expands your well-being.

Larry L. Liberty, Ph.D.
Carmichael, California
July, 1994

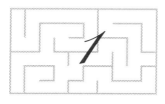

A MODEL

The opportunity to train, consult, coach, and work with thousands of supervisors, managers, and executives has been an exciting one. Though there have been times when I held my head in exasperation, for the most part these people have been generous and committed. This book really began in 1971 when I had my first opportunity to be managed while working for the state government of California.

I was twenty-two and "knew everything". I had spent over a year in Brazil in the Peace Corps and thought that nothing was beyond my limited grasp. It was, almost immediately, a shock to discover that many of these people I had as my managers and supervisors were less than adequate in my humble estimation. It was then, in the summer of 1972, that I began to note the real differences that characterize the best and the worst supervisors and managers.

I made the following notations about supervisors and managers that I had observed:

INEFFECTIVE	EFFECTIVE
Impatient	Patient
Thoughtless	Thoughtful
Inconsiderate	Considerate
Internally Focused	Externally Focused
Self-Centered	Committed to Others
Autocratic	Democratic
Stressed	Had Fun
Disliked from Below	Liked from Below
Tolerated by Peers	Liked by Peers

And so my research began. I could see the obvious differences but I couldn't put them together in a meaningful way. Over the years, I watched and observed many extraordinary supervisors, managers, and executives. Each had their faults and weaknesses. But each had a certain set of qualities that made them extraordinary in the context of their peers and their subordinates. These exceptional leaders include a marketing executive, a communication director, a corporate president, an Army officer, a NASA scientist, a congressman, a dentist, middle managers and an Aikido master. Their personalities vary widely. Their educations range from high school diplomas to doctorate degrees.

Some of these leaders are soft-spoken and some are outspoken, but each has continued to produce extraordinary results — with class and panache in times of stress, confusion, upset, and change. They have each done so with a certain unique ability to pierce to the heart of a matter that needs their attention. For the most part, their internal processes are unconscious and unapparent to them. My joy was to watch, consider, and begin to understand what and how they produced these results.

Over the last eight years I have synthesized the process into an understandable and workable model to allow it to be understood and practiced. Several thousands of people have now worked with the model and the results have been astounding. Here is the model for your consideration and contemplation.

RESULTS

↑

ACTIONS

↑

THINKING

I now believe, having watched successful people in action repeatedly be successful, that results are absolutely correlated to the actions that one takes. I am, at this very moment, moving my fingers and hitting the keys on this keyboard. These actions are producing the specific measurable, observable results that you see in front of you — these words.

Additionally, the question really becomes "how do you create or modify actions to improve results?" In this model your actions are always totally related to the quality of your thinking. You'll notice that you've never done anything that you didn't think about doing ahead of time. Yes, there are times when you do something really wild and you don't know exactly what will be the outcome. But if your friend says "Let's go on a surprise outing. Follow me," and you follow your friend, you have to go through a thought process in order to get to the outing. So the model initially looks like this:

RESULTS   *The outcomes and effects produced are directly correlated to the quality of one's actions taken.*

↑

ACTIONS   *These actions are caused by the quality of the thinking one is able to do at any moment.*

↑

THINKING   *The quality of one's thinking is the key to unlock one's results and ability to handle stress.*

THE QUALITY AND QUANTITY OF YOUR OUTCOMES ARE DIRECTLY RELATED TO YOUR ABILITY TO THINK.

The key to any success in life, especially in business, is the ability to **think**. It is the basis of problem-solving, decision-making, creativity, and vision. It is literally at the heart of whatever actions you ultimately take in interacting with yourself and with your world. What you cannot think about, you cannot work on.

Now this point is critical:

HAVING THOUGHTS IS NOT THE SAME AS THINKING.

All day, every day, from the time we begin to think in words instead of just pictures, we are thinking and we are having thoughts. The distinction here is critical. Webster's Dictionary defines "thinking" as:

> ". . . to bring the intellectual faculties into play; to use the mind for arriving at conclusions, making decisions, drawing inferences, etc.; to perform any mental operation or to reason . . . to conceive . . ."

Are you thinking right at this moment or are you just having some random thoughts float through your head without any purpose or reason? You see, the mind has millions of thoughts each day. Each word that you read on this page is a stimulant and requires your mind to react to it. But what you do with it is really up to you.

Having thoughts is passive. You are not certain how or why the thought got into your head. "Mickey Mantle hit 52 home runs in 1956 . . ." is having a thought, especially if you're standing on a street corner and not speaking to anyone or not thinking about Mickey Mantle or baseball prior to having that thought.

Read the definition of "thinking" from Webster again and ask yourself this question:

Is this definition speaking of something that is active or something that is passive ?

Let me give you some of Webster's other definitions of "thinking" and see whether you think they are active or passive.

"... to intend; to muse; to meditate; to reflect; to weigh something mentally; ... to venture; to call to mind; ... to discover; invent; conceive of; ... to allow oneself to consider ..."

Once again I assert that thinking is different from having thoughts. Thinking is active, dynamic and energetic. Having thoughts goes on throughout your day, and many times you hardly notice or give attention to them unless they stimulate you or upset you somehow.

Now here is the point:

> *IF YOU WANT TO PRODUCE BREAKTHROUGHS IN YOUR RESULTS, YOU HAVE TO LEARN HOW TO HAVE BREAKTHROUGHS IN YOUR ABILITY TO THINK.*

There are two types of stimulants which can provide you with the opportunity to expand your ability to think. Both have to do with expanding your learning.

1. An **idea** that someone else has had (while they were doing some thinking) which causes you to stop . . . and think.

OR

2. A **question** which provokes you to stop and think in new and different ways than you have before.

The key thing that I distilled from watching and observing all of these extraordinary leaders is that they instinctively knew how to ask powerful, penetrating questions.   The key, therefore, is the quality of the questions that you ask yourself, or someone else. If you listen carefully to the questions that great leaders ask, you will notice that they are deeper and more inquisitive about what is really happening. They ask very few rhetorical questions.

Also these leaders who seem to be so wise and able ask very few binary questions, questions that can be answered with a "yes" or a "no". Rather, they ask questions that startle and stop the listener. A great question will, inevitably, stop you in your tracks. It will cause a complete halt to other activities. The question is deep and causes the person responding to go deep into thinking — real thinking.

Leadership and wisdom are integrated in this model.

RESULTS   *The outcomes and effects produced are directly correlated to the quality of one's actions taken.*

↑

ACTIONS   *These actions are caused by the quality of the thinking one is able to do at any moment.*

↑

THINKING   *The quality of one's thinking is the key to unlock one's results and ability to handle stress.*

↑

QUESTIONS   *The quality of one's questions is the key to causing real, powerful, impactive thinking.*

The many supervisors, managers, and executives that I have observed have an intuitive wisdom about them. They can cut to the core of any issue. They can cause people to stop and think — and grow. They can allow themselves to grow, and through it all, they produce extraordinary results.

The key to this process is discovering how to ask questions that matter, to ask questions that cause real, deep, provocative thinking to happen, and to get outside the obvious and inquire about the subtle, the unseen, and the unpredicted. Wisdom is, I believe, a matter of discovering what is really happening and then taking appropriate actions. While it is not possible to absolutely teach someone how to make the correct decision in every case, asking powerful questions generates information and data that leads one closer to a great decision or set of actions.

How to Use This Book

INDIVIDUALS

On the following pages are two different kinds of stimulants to your thinking. Each page has one idea or one thought and one question designed to stimulate your thinking. Some will stop you and you will feel compelled to consider what is written on the page. Some will be meaningless to you . . . at the moment. Some will ring through you like a bell, touching your heart as well as your mind. Some may even irritate you and upset you. Some you may immediately disagree with.

If you are working with this guide as an individual, I recommend the following approach:

1. Find a time and place where you can have peace and quiet for at least fifteen minutes.

2. Select a chapter at random or one that is currently relevant to your situation.

3. Read through the statements until you find one that is interesting and provocative. Don't over analyze this process. Let your intuition select which statement is useful to you.

4. Work with that statement and question until you have made some progress. Write down any notes or thoughts that you have about the topic.

5. Write out a one-line note stating your learning or a question that you have now developed.

6. Make that note visible for a few days. Think about the meaning of the question or statement. Let the process influence you and your actions.

I also strongly recommend that you keep a journal or notebook for your own thoughts, questions, ideas, comments, or reactions. This journal can serve as a baseline for your own development. It is also a great way to capture your thinking in real time. Never underestimate the power of observation, especially when you are observing yourself.

You can, of course, also use the guide in a random fashion. Open it whenever you have a couple of minutes. Let your fingers open whatever page seems to open. Work with whatever you find there at the moment. This approach is also useful and stimulating to the thinking process. In any case, work with the guide over a period of weeks or even months. The depth of the statements and questions can be profound if you let your mind engage fully.

TEAMS

This workbook is, in many ways, one of the most useful team-building tools that you will find. Any group that is trying to become a high-output team is made up of a complex collection of individuals. One of the most difficult teaming issues is the development of understanding and trust between the individuals. This guide is excellent in that context.

I recommend the following types of actions to facilitate

working with teams:

1. Take fifteen minutes at the beginning or ending of each team meeting and discuss a relevant topic. Discuss reactions.

2. Have each member find a specific statement and question which they find useful and provocative. Have each person read them and then discuss why. This will give team members insights into each other.

3. In a variation of the above, you can have the other members give their thoughts and reactions to the statement and question initiated by a member.

4. Pick three specific statements and questions from any of the chapters. Have them identified ahead of time and have each member read and work with the three privately. At a team meeting, have each person describe their learning and what the thinking process was like.

5. In a situation where there is internal conflict between members or there is conflict between two groups, have the members or the groups find the statement and question which, they believe, best moves towards resolution.

6. Have the team leader pick one statement and question for the group to discuss at the opening of a team meeting. Complete the session by having each member say how the opening discussion affected the meeting.

   You will discover new and useful ways for groups and organizations to work with this material. It is intended to facilitate thinking and give people access to their own wisdom and the wisdom of others.

The world is filled with upset, pain, and sadness. It is also filled with joy, creativity, excitement, and vitality. The emotional and mental state one finds oneself in is more determined by what goes on in one's thinking than what is actually out in the world. My belief is that now, more than ever, we need men and women who can stop, think, and act in new, innovative, and bold ways. I hope this text provides some of those moments to you.

INDIVIDUAL CHARACTER

This section is devoted to the issues of character: its development, qualities, and constitution. Character is at the heart of an individual's future since limitation or inhibitions of one's character can filter and color what is possible. Character affects how one sees the world. It is the home of integrity. Character is the well from which most of our other attributes spring.

These pages are designed to assist you in looking into yourself and into your own character. This is a difficult struggle for most of us since we hope that who we are is sufficient, able, and competent. Read these next pages with an eye and ear on honestly looking into your own character and you will benefit from your own honest inquiry.

The noise that you often hear

is you, trying to look and act

important. Really important

people never need to do

anything to show their

importance.

Q

What percentage of your time
do you spend listening and what
percentage of your time do you
spend speaking?

The size of your body has

nothing to do with whether

or not you're an adult.

Q: What do you use to determine
whether you or someone else is
actually mature?

Maturity is the prize of becoming a fully functioning adult. It means being able to determine accurate from inaccurate, and effective from ineffective, without regard for public opinion.

Q

How do you define real maturity, and how would you assess yourself in terms of being mature?

Maturity is related to and caused by many things, but real, expanding maturity is ultimately rooted in listening.

Q: If maturity is rooted in listening, what is your assessment of your ability to really listen, especially when you think you have something important to say?

If you're going to be poor, broke, or out of work, it is always better to be poor, broke, or out of work around people who consider these circumstances to be an opportunity to grow and to learn.

What kinds of people do you have surrounding you?

*You are a speck in the
universe. You are the only
person who really cares
about all of the things that
you care about. If you will
take time to notice, the
universe is totally indifferent.
Now, for some people this is
an upsetting discovery. For
some people, it is the key to
total freedom.*

*Q: What allows one person
to use this information to grow
and another person to use this
information to die?*

Every change in life

represents a test of your

character.

How are you doing on this test?

Patience is more about

trusting yourself than

anything else.

Q: Do you tend to be patient
or impatient and how does this
reflect on your trust of yourself?

Accidents happen. When they do happen you can shrink, rage, blame, or learn. One of these is the prevention of future accidents.

Q

What is your normal response to an accident and how does it affect you and those around you?

The world is filled with

people who want to vote on

whether you are "okay" or

"not okay" as a person. Stop

counting their votes and vote

for yourself.

Q: Who determines whether
you are okay or not?

Participation

is the key to excitement.

Q

What makes people want to participate?

Your ability to accept your

fears and frustrations will

determine the rate at which

you get beyond them.

Q: When you are confronting your frustration and fear, do you look at it directly or do you try to avoid it and get around it as soon as possible?

Honesty and openness are both personal choices.

Q

Under which kinds of circumstances do you choose not to be honest and open?

There is a real difference

between self-confidence and

arrogance. Arrogance is an

expression based in fear.

Confidence is one based in

certainty and discovery.

Q: What activates your arrogance and when does it usually occur?

Buzzwords are no substitute

for honest excitement,

enthusiasm, and

commitment.

What impact do buzzwords, slogans, banners, and programs have upon a person's excitement, enthusiasm, and commitment?

How you see a "problem"

will give you great insight

into what you are afraid of.

Q: What is your biggest problem at this moment and how do you see it and relate to it?

Regarding your standards:

You either live up or you

give up.

Q

When do you give up ?

Ultimately, who you are is

more important than what

you do.

**Q: How often do you consider
your character and make-up,
and then take steps to deepen
yourself and who you are ?**

It is easier to be negative and cynical than to be positive. Being positive comes from self-respect and trust in one's self.

Q

When you are negative and cynical, what have you succumbed to?

Never mistake honesty,

compassion, listening or

caring for weakness.

Q: What are your immediate thoughts and reactions when you interact with someone who has these traits?

Beware of people smiling at you and telling you that things are going fine when your intuition and your heart say otherwise.

Q

How do you determine when to trust yourself and when not to?

There are certain things that

are unavoidable in your life.

The sooner you understand

that, the sooner you can stop

trying to manage the

inevitable.

Q: Are you the kind of person who tries to manage and control what is outside of your control?

Assume ignorance — not malice. Maybe people aren't really out to make your life miserable.

Why would you ever assume malice in the first place?

Maturity is the ability to be

aware of and responsible for

your real impact upon

others.

Q: What is your impact upon others?

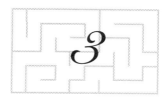

COMMUNICATION

Communication is, obviously, at the heart of effectiveness in any setting. Ask any ten people to identify the most common organizational problems and eight will say communication. But, at it's heart, communication is more than just speaking and being understood.

It is about clarity of thinking, willingness to listen, and the desire to see what someone else sees, exactly the way that they see things. It rests upon generosity and courage as much as skill. Use these pages to carve out a new understanding and appreciation of the importance and power of real communication.

If you're speaking, it is useful

to determine if anyone has

any real interest in listening

to you, or are they just

mannequins looking

interested?

What would have to happen for people to really listen to each other?

People love to speak and to express themselves, whether what they are saying is useful or not.

Q: How do you know if you have something worth saying? What is your test?

The trick in life is to stop talking and speaking endlessly about things when we have nothing to say.

Q

Is there a pattern as to when you find yourself with an opinion or something to say about a topic that you are ill-informed about?

Empowerment is caused by

the amount of responsibility

within any given

conversation.

Q: How do responsibility and empowerment affect each other?

What you think that you

have heard and seen seems

much more important than

what is actually happening.

Q

How is perception a factor in communicating and producing results?

Without your judgments,

evaluations, assessments,

and opinions, many of

which are ill-founded, what

would you talk about ?

Q: What percentage of what you say are your judgments, evaluations, assessments, and opinions?

Listening is ten times more

important than speaking.

Q

Why?

Liberty's Law

YOUR POWER IN LIFE
IS DIRECTLY CORRELATED TO
THE NUMBER OF POSSIBILITIES
YOU HAVE ACCESS TO.

Possibilities, options, and potentialities are multiplied in an environment of clear, honest, direct, and open communications. Without a safe environment in which this is normal, your power is limited dramatically.

How would you assess the quality of the communications within your organizations?

What most people call

"communication" is two or

more people talking at each

other, saying the same things

over and over.

Q: When you feel frustrated in a communication, what is happening in the environment and within you?

Most of what you'll hear at a meeting, conference, or workshop is not something said by the speaker or leader. It is what you'll say to yourself about what that person has said. What you say to yourself about what a person has said to you is what you usually listen to.

Q

What voice is louder when you're at a meeting: the speaker's or the one in your head evaluating the speaker's comments?

Liberty's Law

LISTEN TO DISCOVER!

If you want to find out

something that you don't

know or you need to know,

you have to create a quiet

place inside your head and

then you have to reach out

to find what others are

saying. This is an active

state — a state of intention

and focus — and not a

passive state.

What would have to happen for you to really listen?

Quality communication

always requires three things:

1. Create a context in which

safe communication can

occur.

2. Communicate the needed

content.

3. Complete the conversation

by acknowledging and

recognizing people who

contributed.

Q: Which of these do you do well and which do you do poorly?

In organizations, most communications of importance are filtered through the fear of those who feel they have the most to lose. The result is communication that lacks clarity, precision, and accuracy. Thus, the average employee is left to speculate, interpret, and generally make up the meaning intended from the top of the organization.

What can you do to ensure that important communications are not distorted before they reach the people who need them the most?

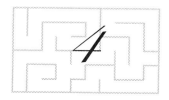

LEARNING & DEVELOPMENT

As we go through life, especially in the world of work, we learn and grow. For many people, however, this pattern of growth and development slows, often to a complete stop. Growing, changing, advancing, and enhancing oneself takes fortitude and courage. Growth does not happen randomly or accidently. It is, most often, the result of conscious effort and determination.

I have developed this section to explore the nature of learning and development. I want to shake up your thinking about the topic and re-design your commitment to it. Your future depends upon it. Your future depends upon your willingness to keep looking, growing, and changing, even when it's difficult and hard. Sometimes the process will be painful and slow. But, with persistence, your own learning and development can leap forward massive distances, effortlessly and elegantly.

Every experience is an opportunity to learn and to grow. If you don't learn and grow from your experience, don't blame the experience.

Q

What facilitates or inhibits your ability to learn from any particular experience?

Most people don't learn

much from their failures.

They are too busy justifying,

rationalizing or denying

them.

Q: When you have a break-down, is your first instinct to be responsible and discover the cause, or to defend yourself?

All of the people who you distrust, hate, loathe, despise, etc., are all part of your opportunity to learn to be an adult.

If you don't consider these people as part of your opportunity to learn to be an adult, what does that say about you?

Coaching requires much more from a person than just being a supervisor or, for that matter, just being supervised.

Q: What does coaching mean to you, and how is that meaning shifting over time?

Renewal is a critical and essential part of any ongoing progress.

Q

What is the nature of renewal?

"Diversity" can either be a program which focuses on changing how a given population looks, or it can be a new way of listening to people who don't seem to look alike.

Q: How many programs do you have that don't get to the substance of what could make them really useful? Why?

You've got to train yourself not to take anything personally. It is hard work because the world you live in is so personal to you. But that is the case for everyone else, too. They're not reacting to you. They're reacting to whatever and whoever stimulates them in their world.

When you take things personally, how does it disrupt your life and the lives of those around you?

Liberty's Law

DON'T TAKE ANYTHING PERSONALLY!

The development process for most adults slows down as soon as they get a full time job that they experience as being "secure". It's not that they want to stop learning, growing and developing. It's that the mind says that it's time to take a break from the discomfort.

What have you consciously or unconsciously done that has inhibited or slowed down your chance to learn and grow?

Learning and development have to do with being able to use old and new information to generate possibilities. Your test of your own development at any moment in time is how many new possibilities you can generate from your cumulative learning.

Q: When you run into a new problem, how does it stimulate or inhibit your growth and development?

Whenever we confront a new, unforeseen, and unfamiliar problem, we typically have three initial reactions: First, we ignore it and deny it, hoping that it will go away. Second, we blame its cause and its solution on someone else, like the government. And third, we modify the definition, complexity, or nature of the problem to fit into the world as we know it, thus giving us a corrupted belief of how to solve it.

What is actually required is that we evolve—in our thinking, our understanding, and our wisdom. Nothing else will do.

How do you react when confronted with a new problem that you have no prior familiarity with, learning about, or understanding of ?

Remember how learning

was for you as a kid?

Q

How has that changed or remained the same for you?

The best way to learn, for

most people, is in a game or

while having fun. The other

way to learn is through

stress, drama, and tragedy.

One is easier than the other.

Q: Under which conditions do
you learn most effectively?

Organizational training and development processes can either treat adults like adults or like children. In one case you will expand learning exponentially. In the other it will seem like climbing a mountain carrying a coffin.

How is your organizational training and development process designed and run?

Individuals are limited in what and how they can learn. The limitations are grounded in their own beliefs, interpretations, and assumptions about what is "true" and what is "real".

Q: *If you wanted to get beyond your own limitations regarding what and how you can learn, who would you ask to assist you and what would you ask them to do?*

Your learning and your comfort are inversely correlated.

Q

What does this mean and how does it impact your learning?

MOTIVATION

At some age we become "mature". This may mean that we're advanced mentally and emotionally, or it may mean we've just gotten older. I believe that real maturity, the ability to act consciously and responsibly, and to deal with the world we live in, has much to do with our understanding of "motivation."

In fact, I believe the words are inextricably tied together. As you investigate this section you will have the chance to look into yourself in the area of motivation, and ultimately your own maturity. You may not agree with all that you read, but keep noticing your internal reactions and discover if they represent those of a fully developed and prepared person, or someone who has more work to do.

There is no training given to us on how to be and act mature. All you have in life are the role models that you have chosen. Unfortunately, if you choose the wrong ones, you won't know it until it is too late. Your access to your own internal motivation is related to your ability to tap into your own maturity.

Who are your conscious and unconscious role models, and which role models would best serve you now?

People work for various

reasons:

▶ *Survival*

▶ *Contribution/Service*

▶ *Approval*

▶ *Fun*

▶ *Pride*

▶ *Joy*

Q: What gets you up in the morning to go to work?

If you want people to act

with integrity in business you

cannot keep changing:

- ▶ *Rewards structures*

- ▶ *Resourcing processes*

- ▶ *Recognition approaches*

How often do you change these and what are the real impacts of these changes upon your people?

Liberty's Law

THE ONLY PERSON YOU CAN
MANAGE IS YOURSELF.

Leadership WISDOM

Ultimately, since the only person you can manage is yourself, the only person you can motivate is yourself.

Q

How does this affect our traditional notions about "motivating" employees?

Integrity is an individual

issue. Organizations create

environments which either

enable or test integrity.

Because we are human,

when we fail a test, most of

us feel bad. We usually

want to share our pain with

our business, or worse yet,

with our customers.

Q: What kind of context does your organization create around the issue of individual integrity?

The problem with hidden agendas is that ultimately, to achieve them, you have to be revealed as having a hidden agenda.

Q

What is the impact upon you when you discover or consider that someone has a hidden agenda?

Inspiration and vision are at

the heart of commitment.

Q: What allows you to feel and express your commitment?

We live in a society that tends

to reward great speakers more

quickly and extensively than

great listeners.

Q

How do you support or contradict
this tendency in your actions and
in your speaking?

Beyond being paid, every
employee is ultimately looking
for two things:

▸ The opportunity to feel like
  they really make a
  difference.

▸ A place to work where they
  feel special and can fiercely
  commit themselves and
  their energy.

*Q: What are you doing to ensure
that your employees can get access
to these two things?*

You'll drive yourself crazy with:

▸ *Being compulsive or,*

▸ *Being lazy*

Given human nature, people who are compulsive are often people trying to overcome the fear that they're really lazy underneath it all. People who are lazy have an internal belief that nothing makes any difference.

How do you respond when you feel compulsive or lazy?

There is no such thing as

"motivating someone". You

cannot motivate another

person. You can excite them

with language, visual

images, or direct experience,

but in the end, motivation is

completely internal to each

individual.

Q: What motivates you to take action and produce results?

We often make the mistake of assuming that what motivates and excites us will do the same for others. Worse, we assume that people are, in general, about the same. That, more than anything, destroys the environment in which people can generate their own participation, action, and results.

What generalizations have you made and do you have about what motivates, energizes, and ignites people to action?

Pure arrogance is telling other people how to get themselves motivated, excited, and into action. It would be far more useful to help them look and discover for themselves.

Q: What questions would allow people to look and discover what motivates, ignites, and excites them to action?

People perform at one of

four levels:

RESIGNATION:

They do almost nothing

because everything seems

hopeless and nothing

matters.

OBLIGATION:

People perform at the

minimally required level and

nothing higher. They will try

to erode that standard further

over time.

INTEREST:

Their learning and results will improve over time as long as their interest is high or growing. If their interest falls off, their performance will soon follow.

COMMITMENT:

People operate out of the motivation to keep their promise to themselves or to someone else. This promise is unconditional — no obstacle will stop them.

Not every job or every task needs a person to be in "commitment" in order to be accomplished.

Q

Which tasks and jobs require real commitment and which can be accomplished in either "interest" or "obligation"?

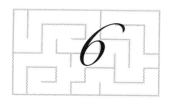

LEADERSHIP

Few ideas or concepts concern research, study, and training more than "leadership". It is an age-old topic with contemporary twists and turns. But this topic needs to be examined deeply from as many perspectives as possible. We too often confuse "leadership" with the position that a person of high rank occupies.

Often those who provide the most leadership in our organizations are of modest level and education. How is this possible? In this set of statements and questions I ask you to explore the meaning of leadership from different angles and viewpoints. In doing so I believe your own leadership character and quality will be deepened.

Leadership is the ability to

bring out "the best" in others

and in ourselves.

Q

How would you assess your leadership ability against this definition?

Management level within an organization and leadership are not correlated.

Sometimes people providing the most leadership are at the lowest levels of an organization.

Q: How does this notion apply to your organization?

*Management and leadership
are really 80% about
creating context for people
to do great work, and 20%
about other stuff.*

Q

*What percentage of your time
do you spend in creating the
context for people to do great
work?*

Risk is filled with unknown

and potential loss. If there is

no unknown or no potential

for loss, then there is no risk.

Q: Where are you risking something significant in your work life or personal life right now?

Moving backward infers that there is or was movement forward.

Leadership is about reminding yourself and others of this process.

When you feel like you're moving backward, how do you usually respond and what impact do you have upon others?

"Opportunity" is an opening

in time that will soon close.

Most people spend their

lives bemoaning the last

opportunity that they missed

. . . instead of preparing for

the next opportunity that is

yet unseen.

Q: What is the role of management and leadership with regard to seeing and accessing "opportunities"?

The more "right" ways you can find, the more likely you'll find a way that will work for more people.

When addressing a new problem or issue, do you typically look for as many effective ways of resolving it as possible, or do you focus on finding the quickest, most expedient solution?

Rejuvenating the human spirit is the job of management. Rejuvenating the human spirit is the result of leadership. It is the doorway to productivity — rejuvenated employees are the most productive employees.

Q: *How do you spend your time, and how much of your time is spent rejuvenating the human spirit at work ?*

Testing is more powerful

than manipulation.

Q

How does testing add power and
manipulation deplete power?

Context is the power to

create meaning out of

events. Given the

opportunity to control

content or influence context,

context-setting will always

be more powerful.

Q: What is the power of concentrating on creating context?

Safety is a more powerful factor in long-term productivity than manipulation or force.

What are you doing to make it safe for the people who work around you?

Managing by using guilt

always produces negative

side effects . . .

- ▶ *Resentment*

- ▶ *Distrust*

- ▶ *Disloyalty*

- ▶ *Covert Hostility*

While all are problems,

covert hostility will express

itself in sabotage, vandalism,

and treason.

Q: What causes people to use
guilt as a management tool?

A strong, calm, gentle

persistence will move things

along more rapidly than

brute force or sheer will.

Q

**Which of these two approaches
is more natural to you and what
changes do you need to make?**

Great technicians manage

content. Great supervisors

manage process, priorities and

content. Great managers

create environments (context)

in which people can manifest

their greatness.

Q: How great are you — given
the job you have to do?

Leadership is about providing an environment that either contributes to the sanity or the insanity of your people.

Q

Are you contributing to the sanity or the insanity of the people around you?

Effectiveness is determined

by a manager's ability to

manage three things

simultaneously:

- ▶ *Results*
- ▶ *Well-being*
- ▶ *Integrity*

Q: Which do you place the most and the least attention on?

Power is not the same as force. Power reveals and releases energy. Force constrains and depletes energy.

Q

What is the role of leadership with regard to using "power" and "force"?

A breakthrough is something

that happens that is positive

and was not supposed to

happen.

Q: When you have a break-through, what actions can you take to ensure that it endures?

Quality is not something you put into your work force, it is something that you bring out in them.

Q

How do you, inadvertently, become a barrier to your people fully expressing their mastery of quality?

Liberty's Law

THE CHARACTERISTICS OF FOLLOWERSHIP AND LEADERSHIP ARE ONE AND THE SAME.

A great way to train leaders to lead is to have them master the process and world of following. This will give them more insight, compassion, and understanding about leading than fifty M.B.A.'s will.

Q

How do you train your leaders, and how does "followership" factor into the learning equation?

RESPONSIBILITY

Responsibility is at the heart of producing results. Through the ages, those people who held their dreams firmly and kept being responsible created far better results than those who blamed, whined, or resigned. Too often responsibility is confused with burden or weight. True responsibility is none of that. It is, I believe, weightless because it is rooted in truth and in choice.

These two elements, truth and choice, are in combination, a powerful chemistry with regard to outcomes and results. Look at these questions and statements to open up new understandings and appreciations of responsibility. Perhaps you may lose weight in the process.

Your greatness is always

determined by your

willingness to:

▶ *Have no hidden agenda*

▶ *Not be attached to your past*

▶ *Create and hold a vision of*

  what is possible

▶ *Give and accept contributions*

How would you rate yourself in these four areas if you were being totally honest?

If your dreams have dimmed

and your heart is timid, and

you have neutralized

everything that you feel in

order to achieve the "good

life", there are two names for

you:

- ▶ *normal*

- ▶ *fool*

Q: What would have to happen within you in order for you to re-create your dreams and re-excite your heart?

Most of your strongest emotional reactions have a hidden agenda to manipulate those around you.

Q

How do emotional reactions, agendas, and manipulations fit together?

Almost no one is really

responding to just YOU.

They are mostly just reacting

to their own past experiences.

Q: How would you behave if you stopped reacting to people as if they were only reacting to you?

Have you noticed that the

most common thing about

all of your personal

problems is . . . you.

Q

Who do you usually blame for your personal problems, or who do you tell yourself is really the cause of most of them ?

After quietly listening to all

of your critics, always thank

them and then go do what

must be done.

Q: How do you respond and react when you come under criticism or receive adverse feedback?

Most people live with the mistaken idea that they couldn't get a better, happier, more fun job. They act as if getting the one they have now was like winning the lottery . . . It wasn't!

Q

How do you relate to the current circumstances in your life?

Responsibility takes more

courage than facing danger.

Q: Why does being responsible take courage?

The more information that you have, the more choices you have. This is why some people avoid the truth and reality like the plague.

Q

How do you deal with new information when the current information has allowed you to come to a firm conclusion?

When the only voice you

can hear and believe is your

own, you're about to

become close friends with a

blind fool.

Q: When you think you are
absolutely certain of something,
what would have to happen to
allow you to become open to
other possibilities?

The major roles of a great
leader include being able to
train, to oversee, to facilitate,
to coach, to focus, and to
acknowledge.

Q

Which of these are your strengths and which of these are not?

The major roles of a great manager are to:

▶ *Create a context in which excellence can grow*

▶ *Bring out the best in themselves and in others*

▶ *Be a role model for the extraordinary*

▶ *Demonstrate the power of vision, enthusiasm and integrity*

▶ *Acknowledge and recognize extraordinary work and effort*

Q: Which of these are natural to you and which are difficult for you?

Procrastination is an attempt to dominate your circumstances through inaction. The paradox is that the only one who is dominated, controlled, and disabled by your inaction is YOU.

Q

To stop procrastinating, what do you have to be responsible for?

"Responsibility" literally means the ability to respond. The less responsible you are, the less ability you have to respond. When you blame someone instead of being responsible, you are giving your ability to respond away. This is the source of your power.

Q: At your best and at your worst, how responsible are you?

Your truth and the truth are

not always the same.

Q

Why are you so attached to believing that what you think is true must be true for everyone?

Acknowledging and accepting

your incompetence is the first

step to learning.

Q: What is your normal first reaction when you discover that you are incompetent in an area?

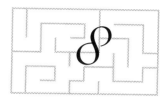

RESULTS

Most often people think of results as the outcome that some boss or organization wants. In fact, it includes those that you, the implementor or catalyst, want. Results happen all the time. You always get results. It's just that sometimes what you said you wanted and what you actually got are very different.

This section looks into the arena of results from many different perspectives. Notice your own orientation to results. If you are thinking one-dimensionally, you may be confused as to why certain statements and questions are here instead of someplace else. Use these statements and questions to expand your ability to produce the results that you really want.

The kind of value that you

get from having insights and

new awareness is very

different from the value that

you get from taking actions.

Q

**In general, what is the value of
a great insight?**

Try this experiment. Write down three things that you know that you want to accomplish. Now, begin to turn the volume down on your internal conversation and go get them done. Just go do them. At the end, ask yourself this question:

Q: How has my internal dialogue changed from the moment I wrote these things down to the moment I completed them?

Being organized and being able to act after being organized are separate but requisite capabilities for success.

Q

Which of these two is easier for you, and which of these needs development and why?

You have a specific amount of attention to use on any given day. You can use your attention to deal with small, insignificant issues or important ones. In either case, when your attention is used up, you won't be able to do anything but go to sleep, even if your body seems to still be awake.

Q: On any given day, do you use most of your attention on important issues or on small, insignificant ones?

Nothing is more powerful

than a great idea implemented

by committed people.

Q

In your work environment, which of these is usually missing?

No movement = no resistance

No resistance = no change

No change = no progress

Q: When circumstances become barriers, what internal conversations do you have and how do they affect you?

People always compare

what is said to what is done;

given how most people

operate, that is totally

appropriate.

What are your standards for determining the validity and integrity of yourself and the people around you?

"Programs" seem to always come into existence in even-numbered years and disappear quietly in odd-numbered years.

Q: What is the difference between a "program" and an initiative which produces lasting results?

Like it or not, it is easier for most people to talk about how to act than it is to demonstrate how to act through their behaviors.

Q

What is the relationship between your actions and your speaking?

If you need to produce a breakthrough in results, you need a breakthrough in actions. Doing the same old things over and over and over again will never produce breakthrough results.

Q: When you need a new result, what will you normally do?

Anyone can be modestly

productive.

Q

Relative to your own standards for yourself, how productive are you?

Managing parts never

produces extraordinary

results.

*Q: What forces are in play
that drive you to manage parts
instead of the whole?*

Your success is ultimately tied directly to the kind of people you surround yourself with . . . that includes those voices inside of your head.

Q

What do the voices inside of your head say about this?

The quantity of rumors and gossip is indirectly correlated to the quality and quantity of the work output at any given time.

Q: Are the rumors more potent than the results in your organization? Sometimes what you don't say is more important and speaks more loudly than what you do say.

On an airplane wing, a small trim tab is as influential and potent as the entire wing.

Q

How does this apply to people producing results?

YOUR truth is often different

than THE truth.

Q: What happens when your truth conflicts with another truth?

What seems impossible to

you . . . IS.

Q

How do you determine what is
possible or impossible in your
life?

People often substitute their

justifications and rationalizations

for the results that they didn't

produce.

Q: What would be a powerful way of acting and behaving if you were unable to produce a result that you had promised?

The beginning of breakthrough results is movement, of any kind. Movement leads to motion. Motion leads to change, and change is the gatekeeper of progress and invention.

No movement = no breakthroughs.

Q

What happens inside of you that prevents you from maintaining movement and motion?

The possibility of "failure" is

what creates the possibility

of success.

Q: How do you relate to the possibility of "failure"?

THINKING

Of all the topics in this text, thinking is at the heart of what gives the other topics power. Thinking and having thoughts are distant cousins. They are in the same family but not really made from the same substance and they produce far different results.

The quality and quantity of the outcomes in your life are related to your ability to think. Whether you are a manager, a parent, an hourly worker, or a scientist — thinking is at the heart of what makes you special. Your special contribution to your job, co-workers, family, and friends, and ultimately to yourself, is created through your ability to think.

Have you ever noticed that just before you feel really tired, angry, or excited, etc., is the thought "I'm feeling really tired, angry, or excited, etc . . ."

Q

Don't you wonder if, just maybe, your emotions are created by your thoughts?

Your life will be determined

by what you think rather

than by what you say.

Q: How is it possible that your thinking is more of a determiner of your life than what comes out of your mouth?   Ultimately, what you say will be determined by what you think anyway.

What most people do with things they cannot understand is to misunderstand it and tell themselves that they now understand what they actually don't understand.

Understand?

Trust is too often based

solely on our past histories

and memories rather than

on the current events.

Q: When you consider trust, is it based more on your experiences of the past or on what is happening in the present?

Thinking usually requires little or no physical movement. If you pay people to think, measure the quality of their ideas instead of how busy they look.

Q

What do you believe "thinking" should look like?

Decision-making should

be made as close to the

customer as possible.

Q: What determines the loca-
tion and level of decision-making
within your organization?

Power is the number of options, choices, and possibilities that you have access to at any moment in time. This is particularly true of thinking.

Q

What has thinking and the ability to think got to do with your power to achieve results?

▶ *Every solution creates new problems.*

▶ *Every problem brings new solutions.*

▶ *Every solution creates new problems.*

▶ *Every problem brings new solutions.*

The trick is to keep sight of the big picture. This allows you to understand and be responsible for the impact that you are having.

Q: Where do you get stuck?

We can never solve world hunger! Don't you agree?

"Zero defects" is unattainable. Don't you agree?

There will never be a total cure for cancer! Don't you agree?

There will never be world peace! Don't you agree?

The Russians will always be our enemies! Don't you agree?

The world is flat. Don't you agree?

The earth is the center of the universe. Don't you agree?

Thinking for yourself is more difficult if everyone around you agrees that a particular way of thinking is correct.

How do you know that you are thinking for yourself?

How do you know when

you're actually thinking?

Q

How do you actually know?

The mind is like a complex filing system. Everything that you have ever seen, heard, touched, smelled, tasted, or experienced in any way is part of your file system. Also, unless you have physical damage to your brain, your brain is capable of remembering anything. ANYTHING! The problem, of course, is that you often don't have the access codes.

Q: What do you think about your mind, how it works, and what potential it holds?

The fastest way to make people crazy is to leave them uncertain, unsafe, or in a condition of unpredictability. The mind, upon encountering these experiences, will try to solve the problem by creating certainty, stability, predictability and safety, even where none may be available. This is the beginning condition of insanity for most people.

Q: What are you and your organization doing that is either creating or preventing certainty, stability, predictability, and safety for your employees?

Do you know why many people love to gossip? It's simple. People love to gossip because:

1. *The mind loves drama, excitement, and a good story.*

2. *The mind is always looking for something titillating rather than the mundane and boring things it has to deal with.*

3. People who don't have enough to keep them occupied are looking for problems to solve.

4. The mind can't cope with everything it has to deal with so it looks externally for an avoidance.

Q

What do you do that contributes to and fosters gossip?

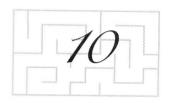

TEAMS

No instrument or resource is more powerful in an organizational setting than a high-performance team. What great individuals cannot accomplish, teams somehow can achieve. It has been this way for years and is more true today. Your ability to discern when and where you need a real team is at the heart of your ultimate productivity. Not every group needs to become a team. But when a team is required, nothing is more powerful, more impactful, and more stunning than the work and experience of being on a team.

In these pages you will find questions and statements designed to cause you to think, engage, and inquire into the nature of teams and into the groups that you now consider to be teams. Use these pages carefully and a new set of dramatic improvements will be available to you.

An easy test of whether a group is actually a "team" is to find out how well the group takes care of and integrates new members. The same rule applies to how former members are treated when they leave.

Q

When you joined your current group, how well taken care of did you feel?

*One of the most powerful
aspects of having a diverse
work force is to have access
to new, unique perspectives
and ways of thinking. There
is power in creating new
possible solutions.*

**Q: How do the concepts of
"diversity" and creating a real
high-output team go together?**

A real team is, by nature, inclusive. Any group that is exclusive is, by nature, not a real team.

Q

In the groups that you are a key member of, is the nature to be inclusive or exclusive?

Representation is the key to

creating a real team.

Q: When a member of your team is out alone, do you trust them to represent the entire team?

Partnership and leadership

are siblings.

Q

What does this mean in the context of the teams that you are a part of?

Everything you do and say,

every action and word, is in

some way a public expres-

sion of who you are.

Q: How does this notion apply within a team?

There is an inordinately

higher amount of teams than

there is "teamwork".

Q

How much teamwork does your group generate?

There is a paradox in teams:

The greater the diversity of thinking, the more difficult it becomes to fully use the power of that diversity.

Q: How do your group's communication skills impact the group's ability to fully use its diversity of thinking?

Teams have the capacity and yearning for breakthroughs. If you need to create a breakthrough result, you need a real team.

Q

Where do you need a real team to produce a breakthrough?

Groups and teams are as different as birds and bees. They have a few things in common but, for the most part, their differences are more striking than their similarities.

Q: What are the key differences between teams and groups?

Not every group needs to be a team. Save yourself some money, some time, and some of your employees' good will. Don't do "Team Building" unless you need a breakthrough result and all of the members of the group have the same goal.

Q

Where do you have groups that need to be teams, and groups where it seems unnecessary to be teams?

The next time someone tells

you that a group needs to be

a "team" ask them why? If

they don't say anything

about needing an

extraordinary result and a

commonality of goal, then

the group doesn't really need

to be a team.

Q: Why are we so enamored with having to create teams anyway?

There are four absolutely essential elements of creating a real high-performance team. In this order you need to ensure:

1. A common, clear, and concise goal for all members.

2. An understanding of and agreement about the interdependencies amongst the members.

3.   The opportunity for each team member to grow and develop as part of being on the team.

4.   A common commitment to represent each other.

Regarding your best team, how effectively are these elements in place?

If team members will not actively and consciously represent the total team (instead of themselves and their own personal agendas), breakthrough results are impossible. It takes a special kind of trust, vision, reliance, confidence, and responsibility to be a member of a real team.

How effectively do you and the members of your organization represent the organization instead of just your own personal perspectives, identities, etc.?

Liberty's Law

REPRESENTATION IS THE PATH
TO BREAKTHROUGHS.

When you become a new member of a real team, they will welcome you, include you, make it safe for you, and test you. The test, in a real team, is only a demonstration of their affinity and desire to have you be a member. They never make you pay dues, prove anything, or be a junior partner. There is a simple reason why not—teams are committed to exceptional results and not to history and politics.

How would you describe your entry into a recent group or team in terms of the issues mentioned?

If you ever get the chance to be a member of a real team, you'll never forget it. It is a thing of joy.

Q

What is the source of joy in participating in a real team?

CUSTOMERS / QUALITY

It is now clear that anyone who has no customers has added no value to an organization. It is also clear that what we mean by "quality" differs greatly from corporation to corporation and from individual to individual. Clearly nothing has more impact upon our futures in the long term than the satisfaction of both our internal and external customers.

This section is designed to cause you to examine your current thinking, assumptions, and presumptions about customers and quality. Given the importance of these topics, a regular examination of ourselves and of our understanding of these topics is both wise and prudent.

When job titles and levels are more important than results, employees will pay more attention to job titles and levels than to their customers.

Q

What are you doing to ensure that there is no confusion amongst your employees about your customers being more important than your bureaucracy... Sir, Yes Sir! ! (substitute "Ma'am" as needed)?

Never, ever, have banners,

buttons, and signs that make

your customers laugh . . . at

you.

Q: What are you doing that is embarrassing to your front-line staff?

You are only as effective as

your last interaction with

your customers.

Q

How do you assess and judge the interactions that your organization has with customers, or what do your customers say to each other about interacting with you?

Never have banners,

buttons, and signs that are

impossible for the lowest

level employees to live up to

with your customers.

Q: When you start a new campaign, crusade, or approach, what consideration do you give to how it will impact your employees?

An internal customer is

usually a person who you

have lunch with but who

you would never have over

for dinner.

Q

How do you treat your internal customers compared to your external customers?

Technical knowledge is only as powerful as the technicians' understanding and appreciation of the customer and their needs.

Q: How do you prevent customers from being bored when listening to your technical discussions that are unappreciated except by you?

Downsizing, re-sizing, right-

sizing, and reorganizing all

have the same root cause —

a failure to provide sufficient

value to customers.

Q

**What is the "party line" about
the causes of your initiatives to
downsize, re-size, right-size,
and reorganize?**

Any group that is more

interested in its own survival

and endurance than in the

customers is a bureaucracy.

Q: What kind of group do you work in and why do you think so?

Customers have this strange

kind of loyalty. Most will

stay with a supplier through

good times and tough times

if two simple things happen:

1. *They perceive that they*
    are getting a good value.

2. *They experience that the*
    supplier thinks they are
    special.

What are you doing to make
your customers stay with you?

Ultimately, your employees cannot treat your customers much better than they feel treated.

Q: What are you doing to ensure that your employees feel well-treated?

Customers come in two

flavors:

First, those who are totally

money-conscious. They will

switch their supplier every

day for a better deal.

Second, those who strive for

a long-term relationship built

on value, trust, and the belief

that they are special.

If your business caters to the

first kind of customer, you

will be crazy and broke. If it

caters to the second kind of

customer, and you take care

of them, you will prosper

and enjoy the experience.

What kind of customers are you chasing?

Keep your eyes open and look for the important moments, the moments of truth, with the customer. They come disguised as normal interactions but they are worth ten times as much.

Q

How do you know an important moment when you see one?

The person who usually

knows the most about a

customer is the one who is

closest to the customer.

Too often we promote these

people away from the

customers and assume the

customer will automatically

be taken care of as usual.

Q: Who knows the most about your customers, their needs, their desires, and their changing perceptions?

If you're committed to quality, really committed to it, you ask the question "what happened?" much more often than "why?".

Q

When things go wrong, which of these questions do you ask first and most frequently?

Long term success is a

function of tension-reducing

events more than tension-

causing events. Too much

tension destroys.

Q: What are you doing to manage and create tension-reducing moments for your staff?

The customer never, ever, ever, cares about your internal problems, dramas, tragedies, difficulties, dilemmas, or emergencies.

Q

What do you suppose that customers actually care about?

An expert's mind is usually

filled with answers about

how to make the customers

happy. If your mind is

empty, you might hear

something new.

*Q: When you work with
customers, are you open or do
you consider yourself an expert?*

*Every day customers will
knock on the door and want
to tell you the truth about
your business. Mostly you'll
tell them to go away and not
bother you . . . you're too
busy searching for the truth.*

Q

**When a customer gives you
information that you don't like,
how do you react to it?**

If you don't have any

customers, your position is

of no value.

Q: Who are your customers and how often do you speak with them?

Mediocrity either expands into greatness or degenerates into nothing. When you have customers, you'll always be tested to see if you really want to be great.

Q

Are you moving towards mediocrity or greatness?

VALUES

I have created this section on values because I believe that, for the most part, we neglect reflecting on what our values really are. It is often the case that what we consider to be our values and what our actions demonstrate are contradictory.

Therefore, there is, whether we like it or not, a values conflict. In the world of work, we often find that the easiest way to deal with these conflicts is by not discovering them in the first place. This is short-sighted and, ultimately, filled with more pain and suffering than we can imagine. Use this section to look into yourself and support yourself in operating consistent with your values.

Owning a Rolex watch says that you are able to obtain a Rolex. That's all it says about you. Anything else you think it says is just part of your own personal insanity.

Q

What is really important in your life right now?

Consider this:

Look at the last 24 hours of

your life . . .

Q: Given what an objective outsider might see, what and who would they conclude are your top priorities?

Look at the last week of your

life . . .

Q

Given what an objective outsider might see, what and who would they conclude are your top priorities?

Look at the last month of

your life . . .

Q: *Given what an objective outsider might see, what and who would they conclude are your top priorities?*

Look at the last year of your life . . .

Q

Given what an objective outsider might see, what and who would they conclude are your top priorities?

People who are rich are

usually safer than people

who are famous.

Q: Would you rather be rich or famous, and why?

Many people live as if having fun, ecstasy, passion, love, and excitement in their life requires prior reservations.

Q

Who do you call to make reservations for having fun, ecstasy, passion, love, and excitement in your life?

Perceptions are what you consider to be real. We know that because people are normally more committed to their perceptions than to what is real. They put more value on perception than on reality.

Q: When do you become more committed to your perceptions than to discovering the "truth"?

Fulfillment in life is directly related to contribution. If you want to experience a fulfilling life, you must find ways to contribute.

Q

How often do you experience personal fulfillment, and how does it relate to the concept of contribution?

An organization's future is

determined by its vision, but

ensured by its values.

**Q: How does this apply to you
and your organization?**

If you want to know what you consider to be important in your life, look and see what you have been doing today, yesterday, and the day before.

Q

What do you consider to be important and how is that consistent or inconsistent with what you have been doing for the last few days?

*Recognizing a person's
value and importance is an
expression of the values and
priorities of an organization.
You can tell a lot about the
priorities and values of an
organization by who and
how it recognizes and
rewards its people.*

**Q: How would you assess
your organization's value of its
people and of their importance?**

You will always, always

work on what is important to

you regardless of what you

tell yourself or others.

Q

What causes your actions and words to conflict around what is important to you?

It is easier to commit to

something that you greatly

value. It isn't always

necessary, but it is easier.

Q: Why is it easier?

Leadership WISDOM

232

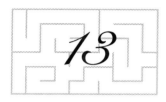

HUMAN BEHAVIOR

The study and understanding of human behavior is at the core of effective supervision and management. Those who focus on only outputs and end results, and ignore the complex set of issues related to the workers, are tempting fate.

This section reflects many of the current thoughts and ideas about human behavior. Whether you agree with a statement or not is less important than your own personal investigation and research into the area.

Anger, hostility, resentment, and aggression are all rooted in fear.

Q

Why would you be angry if you weren't afraid of something?

Worry and doubt can be useful as alarms, as ways of shifting our attention. But, like any real alarm, if you hear it too much you simply adapt to it and stop using it to learn from.

Chronic worry and doubt can also be used to shield our fear.

Q: How much worry and doubt do you live with, and how does this affect you personally?

Since each person has a finite amount of attention, how you use it determines your ultimate success. You can either "major in minors" or "major in majors".

Q

How do you spend your energy and attention during an average day: on minor things or major things?

If you can't speak your mind,

you cannot be yourself. If

you cannot be yourself, you

will never produce

breakthrough results.

Q: What prevents you from speaking your mind and telling, what you consider to be, the truth?   What is that inside of you?

Sometimes the past reveals and offers insights into the future. But sometimes it does not. If you're too attached to the past, you might just be spending your time on the irrelevant.

What is there about your past that seems so attractive and makes you want to attach to it and hold on tight?

Sincerity is only powerful

when accompanied by

sincere actions.

Q: What is the relationship between being sincere and acting sincerely?

Life is a series of different conversations and dialogues that we have with each other and with ourselves.

Q

Which of these conversations and dialogues has the most influence on you?

Our perceptions of "reality"

begin and end with the

thoughts and internal

dialogues we have with

ourselves — especially about

ourselves.

Q: What is your most potent and persistent conversation, perception, dialogue, or discussion that you have with yourself about yourself?

During a training session, the most important conversations that will happen during the day are not between the instructor and the student about the content of the workshop. Rather it is the conversations the students will have with themselves about the workshop.

When you are in a training class, what conversations are the most important to you?

Sometimes what is real isn't as much fun as our perceptions. What most people do is avoid and deny reality . . . it temporarily stops the pain.

Q: What is your normal way of dealing with reality when it is difficult and painful?

Fundamentally people avoid pain and pursue pleasure. This is their operating principle for life. And the "prime directive'" for most people is to AVOID PAIN AT ANY AND ALL COST.

Therefore, the biggest motivator for most people is the desire to avoid and minimize pain.

What is your relationship to avoiding pain and discomfort?

Hostility and anger are

rooted in fear.

*Q: When you are angry and
hostile, what are you afraid of
down underneath all of that?*

Disappointment is based

upon your current level of

expectation.

Q

What is the meaning of the phrase "An expectation is an upset looking for a place to happen"?

Safety creates approachability.

Approachability creates relationship.

Relationship creates intimacy.

Intimacy creates passion.

Q: What does this mean in the context of you and your job?

Anyone or anything that you avoid has an invisible power over you.

Q

What or who are you avoiding, and how does that give them power over you?

The main reasons that "we"

become "us versus them" are

those fears we have which are

based in our own immaturity

and irresponsibility.

Q: When you begin to think from "us versus them", what are you afraid of?

You are not your position.

Q

When your position has not been accepted or has been outright rejected, have you been rejected, and if you think so, what part of you has been rejected?

When you're in a state of

obligation, time stands still.

Q: What internal emotional states does being in obligation create?

Yelling causes tension.

While there are times when

tension can be useful, for the

most part tension caused by

yelling usually turns into

fear.

Q

How do you determine when it is appropriate to yell, speak loudly, or create a level of tension in others?

The human spirit seeks

freedom and responsibility.

Q: What happens to people when their spirit is depressed or covered over?

To trust yourself, your intuition, experiences, and senses, you must first overcome your fear.

Q

What happens that prevents you from trusting yourself?

What you say to yourself

about yourself is much more

important than what others

say or think about you.

Q: What do you most often say about yourself to yourself — about your worth, your quality, your value, your ability, and your competence?

A person whose attention is more on themselves than on you will betray you if the circumstances are not in their favor.

Q

How do you ascertain the location of a person's attention?

When you get bored, you're usually very close to your own creativity.

Unfortunately, many of us cannot allow ourselves to stay bored very long, so the creativity is never uncovered.

Q: When you feel bored, what conversation is inside of your head and how does it affect your actions?

Whatever you attempt to control is controlling you. The joke is that you're usually the last one to know that.

Q

What is the meaning of the phrase: "All control is an illusion"?

Most of the people you meet

are trying to prove something

to themselves or to someone

else. Usually it's too late

anyway.

Q: What are you trying to prove to yourself or others?

The things that you withhold

or avoid become your

demons. They haunt you

until you die or decide to

live.

What are you withholding or avoiding, and why?

What you do (and don't do)

today is determined by what

you consider to be "possible"

and "urgent" tomorrow.

Q: What are you not doing?

OTHER THOUGHTS

I have saved the following uncatagorized ideas, statements, and questions for this section. Approach it as a buffet where you can sample different items without having filled yourself or gone hungry. It covers a variety of issues and should provide you with unique opportunities to test and tune your thinking.

A concept is always just a

partial perception of reality.

Be careful of those who speak

in concepts that are too

simple or too good to be true.

When you have a perception of reality, how do you ensure that it is not incomplete?

Avoiding or denying the truth

will not make it disappear.

Q: How does confronting the truth empower your ability to deal with change?

When you are in a state of

obligation, part of you will

be planning your escape

across the border.

Q

What obligations are you consciously or unconsciously planning to attempt an escape from?

When you are dead, what

will remain?

Q: More importantly, what difference will it make that you lived?

In a world filled with gorillas, it is more useful to learn to dance with them than to hunt unarmed.

Q

What and who are the gorillas in your world?

Business is filled with the paradox:

"Rely on yourself" and "You're part of a team".

Great managers can resolve this paradox.

Q: How do you work with this paradox to support others?

Create your reality or your

reality will create you.

Q

**Who is creating your reality
right at this moment?**

There is always something

far worse.

Q: Given your current situation, what could be worse?

The difference between life

and death is . . . one breath.

Q

Do you live as if every second
and every breath matter?

When you die, all of your

problems will immediately

disappear.

Q: Why are you so surprised?

When you reach the age of

30, it is appropriate to give

up blaming your youth for

what you have today.

**When things aren't going well
and you're upset, who do you
quietly blame?**

You can spend your time

doing three things:

▶ *Reliving the past*

▶ *Experiencing the present*

▶ *Creating the future*

Two of these three will

generate success and one

will drive you insane.

Q: When you feel like you're going insane, where are you spending your time?

Nobody but you cares about your personal problems, issues, barriers, difficulties, and upsets.

Do you ever find that sometimes you don't even care?

Avoid people who cannot

resist the temptation to go

over Niagara Falls just to get

a drink of water.

Q: What is the difference between enthusiasm and being compulsive?

Your life ultimately turns upon:

- ▸ *How well you take care of yourself.*
- ▸ *How well you take care of others.*
- ▸ *How well you let yourself be contributed to.*

How do you handle these things?

Your ultimate ability to know
something happens as you
allow yourself to fully
experience it. Nothing takes
the place of experience and
yet some people keep
creating the same
experiences over and over
again, afraid to let go of
those that are safe and
familiar.

Q: What is the difference
between knowing something
intellectually and experiencing
something directly?

In the end, we will each be known for our results and actions.

What will you be known for?

To Contact The
Liberty Consulting Team:

The Liberty Consulting Team can be reached for workshops, keynote speeches and tailored programs through:

THE LIBERTY CONSULTING TEAM
2120 Shelfield Drive
Carmichael, California 95608
916.484.6463
1.800.333.3LCT

Popular current workshop and presentation titles include:

Multi-Dimensional Thinking
The Architecture of Success
Managing From The Future
Leadership/Followership
Change Management
Creating and Maintaining High-Performance Teams
The Last Listening Workshop

Our consulting services include:

Organizational Development Interventions
TQM Design, Implementation, and Assessment
Team Coaching
Human Systems Reengineering